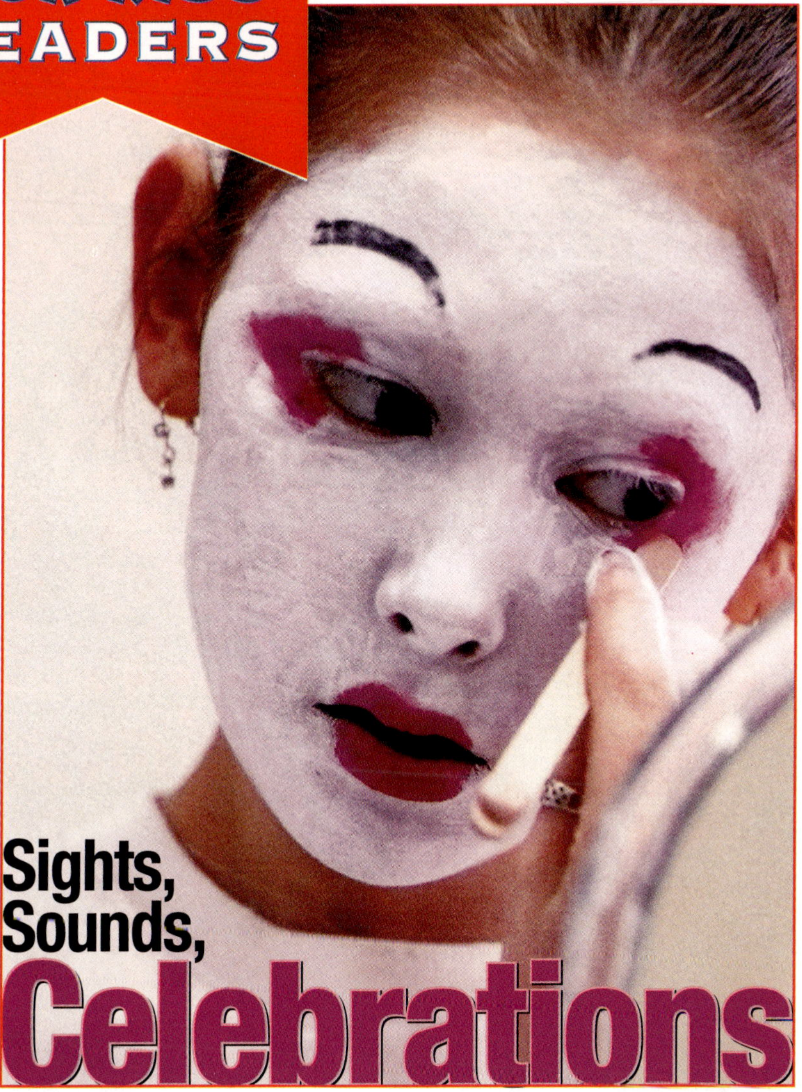

Sights, Sounds, Celebrations

by Jeri Cipriano

Orlando Austin Chicago New York Toronto London San Diego

Visit *The Learning Site!*
www.harcourtschool.com

People everywhere love to sing. They love to dance. Singing and dancing make most people feel good.

Women in India dance in a parade to celebrate a national holiday.

Kabuki

Kabuki is a form of Japanese theater that began 400 years ago. It was started by a woman as a kind of dance. At first, both men and women took part. Then the Japanese rulers decided that women should not appear on stage. Men played all the parts.

Kabuki plays and dances are based on events in history and on everyday life. This art form has special rules. To take part in a Kabuki play or dance, you must come from a family of Kabuki performers or be adopted by one.

Male performers who play female roles are called *onnagata*, which means "woman-persons." They always wear white face cream. They put red color around their eyes and eyebrows.

Kabuki costumes are very heavy. They can weigh up to 40 pounds! Kimonos (Japanese dresses) used in Kabuki are very special. They are made so the performers can change from one character into another with a simple twist or turn of the body.

OPERA

Opera is a kind of drama, or play, that is set to music. In opera, actors do not speak their parts. Instead, they sing and act at the same time. Opera began in Italy in the year 1594.

The idea behind opera was to re-create ancient Greek drama. People knew the words of these early dramas, but no one knew how they had been performed. In Italy, music and song became the main parts of opera.

The Metropolitan Opera House in New York's Lincoln Center is a famous place where operas are performed.

Soon, the love of opera spread to other countries. Today, operas from many years ago are still performed in countries all over the world.

Dance

Since the beginning of time, people have moved their bodies and stamped their feet to the rhythm and sound of music.

A Native American member of the Pueblo tribe performs a buffalo dance at a special ceremony.

Dance shows how people feel. It is used to tell stories, to celebrate things that have happened, or just to have fun. People all over the world love to dance.

These are members of a Korean children's dance group.

Ballet

Even the kings and queens of Europe loved dance. Plays and dances were performed for them in their royal courts.

Ballet began in Italy. However, the first complete ballet was performed in France in 1581. It was created to celebrate a royal wedding. It went on for five and a half hours!

Ballet

In the 1600s, France had the best ballet dancers. French dancers visited other countries to teach their steps. Soon, there were ballet schools in many countries.

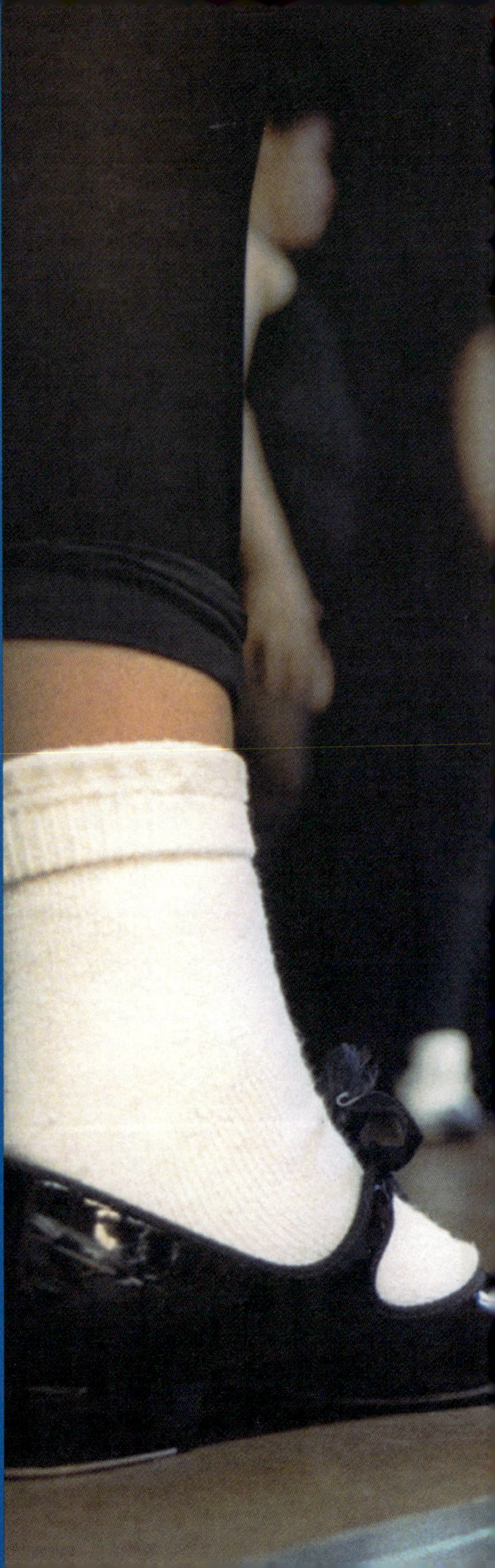

In the United States, more modern forms of dance were created. People used the jazz music of the early 1900s. One dance mixed the Irish jig and the English clog dance with an African dance. This was the beginning of tap dancing.

New dances are created all the time. What are some dances you know?